90422 P

ART FOR KIDS

COMIC STRIPS

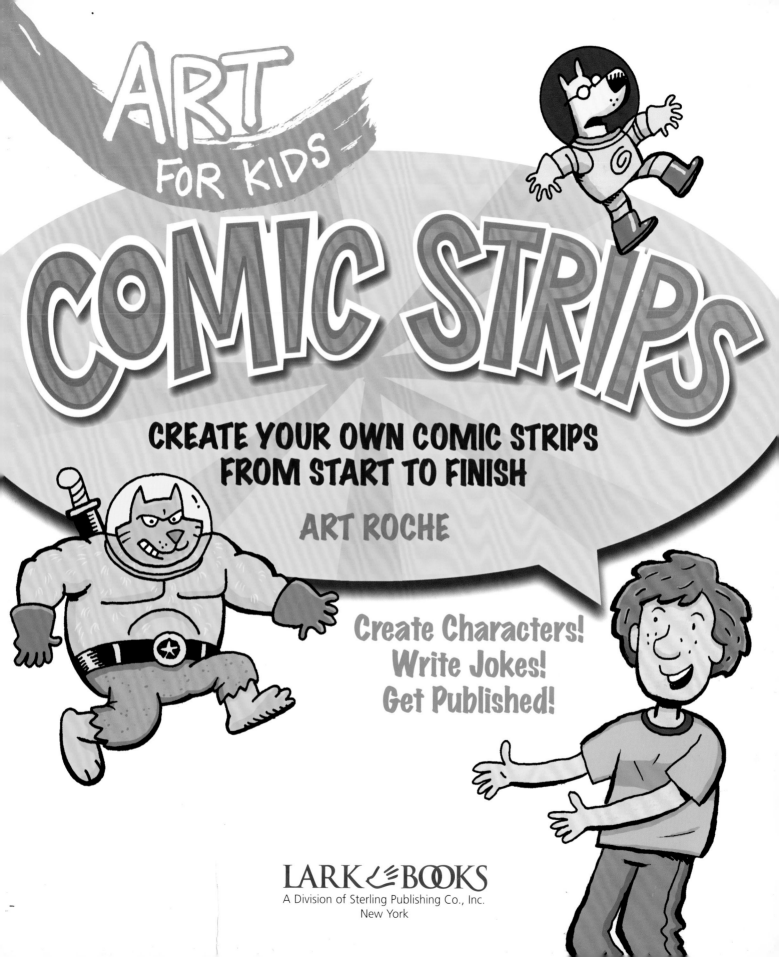

# ART FOR KIDS

# COMIC STRIPS

## CREATE YOUR OWN COMIC STRIPS FROM START TO FINISH

### ART ROCHE

Create Characters!
Write Jokes!
Get Published!

LARK BOOKS
A Division of Sterling Publishing Co., Inc.
New York

**Editor:** Wolf Hoelscher

**Creative Director:** Celia Naranjo

**Design & Production:** Robin Gregory

**Cover Illustration:** Art Roche

**Editorial Assistance:**
Rose McLarney & Delores Gosnell

10 9 8 7 6 5 4 3 2 1

First Edition

Published by Lark Books, A Division of
Sterling Publishing Co., Inc.
387 Park Avenue South, New York, N.Y. 10016

© 2006, Art Roche

Distributed in Canada by Sterling Publishing, c/o Canadian Manda Group, 165 Dufferin
Street, Toronto, Ontario, Canada M6K 3H6

Distributed in the United Kingdom by GMC Distribution Services,
Castle Place, 166 High Street, Lewes, East Sussex, England BN7 1XU

Distributed in Australia by Capricorn Link (Australia) Pty Ltd.,
P.O. Box 704, Windsor, NSW 2756 Australia

If you have questions or comments about this book, please contact:
Lark Books, 67 Broadway, Asheville, NC 28801, (828) 253-0467

Manufactured in China

For information about custom editions, special sales, and premium and corporate
purchases, please contact Sterling Special Sales Department at 800-805-5489 or
specialsales@sterlingpub.com.

# Contents

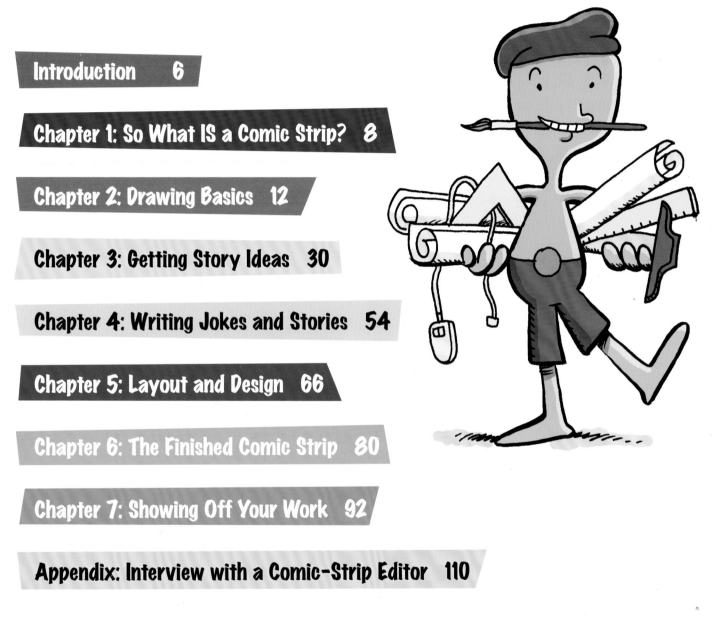

# Introduction

Do you love to draw cartoons? Do you doodle on every scrap of paper you can find? Have you ever thought about creating your very own comic strip? If you answered yes to any of these questions, you've come to the right place.

After 25 years of drawing cartoons and comic strips, I'm pleased to present a book that will explain all the little things that go into creating a comic strip: drawing tips, an introduction to writing jokes and creating characters, and ideas about getting published. This is not your standard, run-of-the-mill "how-to-draw" book. *Art for Kids: Comic Strips* focuses on comic strips, and comic strips only.

# What's Ahead...

The best way for me to show you how to create a comic strip is to do it myself—right before your eyes. By watching me move from rough sketches to final inks, you'll learn about the fun and challenge of creating something brand new and how to avoid any pitfalls along the way. The extra bonus for me is that I get to design a new comic strip and write a book at the same time. That's what I call multitasking.

As an artist creating a comic strip, you can be the writer, the director, the camera operator, and art director all rolled into one. And every cartoonist draws differently—I don't want or expect you to draw the way I do. Part of the fun of your journey through this process is developing your own style. The way you draw your characters should be as unique as your own fingerprints. There is no one right way to cartoon anything. Just have fun!

# Chapter 1
# So What IS a Comic Strip?

A comic strip is a series of cartoons that tell a story. Comic strips are read from left to right, just like a book. And like a book, the best comic strips can tell fantastic stories of adventure, humor, and suspense. The great challenge for the comic-strip artist and writer is to tell these stories in only three or four windows (or panels) at a time.

© King Features Syndicate, Inc.

## The First Comics

By the end of the 19th century, the first comic strips began to appear in U.S. newspapers. It was a time when two powerful newspaper publishers, Joseph Pulitzer and William Randolph Hearst, were competing with each other to get more readers (and more money) for their newspapers. In 1893, Hearst took a risk: he tried running a comic strip in his *San Francisco Examiner* called *The Little Bears*, drawn by artist James Swinnerton. It was a big hit.

Not to be outdone, Pulitzer printed the first color comic in 1895. It was called *The Yellow Kid* and was drawn by Richard F. Outcault. It, too, was wildly successful.

Two years later, Rudolph Dirks debuted *The Katzenjammer Kids* in another Hearst-owned paper. It was the first strip to use speech balloons. In those days, cartoonists were like movie stars. Because there were no TVs, the daily comic strip was great entertainment for the average citizen.

# Comics Grow Up

As years passed, comic strips grew incredibly popular—as popular as movies are today. Although Chic Young's *Blondie* or Elzie C. Segar's *Popeye* were funny, most comic strips of the early 20th century used drama more than comedy.

*Gasoline Alley*, created by Frank King in 1918, became the first family-oriented soap-opera strip. Chester Gould's *Dick Tracy*, a violent detective comic, debuted in 1931. Lee Falk created *The Phantom*, a fantasy-adventure strip, in 1936. *Prince Valiant* by Hal Foster was an epic adventure story that started in 1937.

Comics didn't use a lot of humor until mid-century. In 1950, Charles Schulz's *Peanuts* began to run in papers across the U.S., and it quickly became one of the most popular comic strips ever. It eventually had more than 355 million readers. *Peanuts* paved the way for the many comic strips that followed it. Comics like *Garfield*, *Doonesbury*, *Foxtrot*,

Peanuts: © United Feature Syndicate, Inc.

*Calvin and Hobbes*, and *For Better or For Worse* all use comedy to tell their daily stories. (See my recommended reading list on page 111 for some book collections of these popular cartoons.)

# Are All Comic Strips the Same?

Nope. Today, people from around the world read many types of comics. Most are like the standard three- or four-panel humor comics that you'll see throughout this book. Some tell the continuing story of a set of characters, with each comic acting as the next short chapter in the story. Other humor comics tell daily jokes that could be read in any order. These are called "gag-a-day" comics.

Some comics only appear in the Sunday newspaper. These comics are usually more serious and tell stories that should be read in order. They're like little weekly movies.

What makes comics special is that they can tell all types of stories about all kinds of characters: human or animals, cowboys or cows!

# What Makes a Comic Strip a Comic Strip?

Funny or serious, daily or weekly, all comics are told in a series of sequential boxes, or panels. Each panel represents an instant in time. Strips are read from left to right, with time passing as the reader moves to each new panel. The combination of artwork, text, and time tell a story.

# Chapter 2
# Drawing Basics

## Comic Strip Tools

You don't need any expensive tools to start drawing comic strips. It's best to begin with materials that don't cost a lot of money.

## Erasers

Buy a soft, pink block eraser at an office-supply store. One of these will work fine for most comic strips.

## Pencils

Wooden pencils with #2 lead will work fine. Mechanical pencils with 2B leads are great if you erase as much I do. The lead is soft enough to erase without damaging the paper too much. If you want thin, light lines, try an HB lead.

You might also consider buying some blue-colored pencils, which make cleaning up your drawings a lot easier. I'll say more about these in chapter 6 (page 82).

# Pens

There are a few options for what types of pens you can use to create your final drawings. Just remember that there are:

Fine-tip markers: These draw a nice, even black line. They come in a variety of tip sizes. I mostly use a 0.05 mm size, but experiment with a size that works best for you.

Ballpoint pens: These pens work, too, but sometimes the lines they make can be too thin to photocopy.

Brush-tipped pens: These are basically ink pens with brush-like tips made of fiber. Use a brush-tip pen to create the flowing, thick, and thin line effects around corners.

You can find any of these pens at just about any office-supply store. Any type will work, but you may want to start out with an inexpensive fine-tipped marker. Brush pens will be discussed later on page 84.

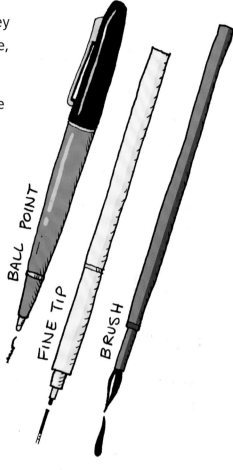

# Paper

Cartoonists are always crumpling up paper and tossing it out. You'll probably be doing the same thing. Nothing's perfect on the first try. So buy a cheap sketchpad—something to carry with you at all times. This is for drawing practice and for jotting down any funny ideas you may have for your cartoon strip. Nothing fancy. You might be making a hook shot with it into the trash can anyway.

Inexpensive printer paper works fine for practice at home. For your finished works, try thicker, 100-pound paper called "Bristol Board." Buy this paper in 11 x 17-inch pads. Another option is to use any pad of art paper called "drawing paper." This paper is usually fine, but don't buy anything that has a very rough surface.

# What's on Your Desk?

Let's look at my cartoonist's desk and talk about some of the other items I use every day.

Most cartoons are drawn 13 inches wide by 4 inches high. If you buy 11 x 17-inch paper, you can turn it sideways and draw two comics on each page. But be sure to draw your cartoons at any size that feels comfortable to you. There's no set rule.

Use a T-square to line things up on your paper. I use one to draw the panels around my strips or to keep the dialogue I write in a straight line.

Tape your paper to the table using masking tape.

A drawing table is fun to have, but you don't really need one until you're serious about cartooning. Until then, the kitchen table can be used just as well. Any flat, clean surface with a straight edge will do.

Use a nice table lamp to illuminate your work surface.

# Starting to Draw

One thing I've learned over the years is to be loose while I draw. Not many professional cartoonists draw something cleanly the first time they touch pencil to paper.

Practice holding the pencil between your thumb and index finger. Drag the pencil back and forth across the paper and make multiple lines for every curve. Don't press down too hard. If you relax and sketch loosely, you can correct little mistakes as you go and decide what looks best as you build up your drawing.

Pretend that you're a sculptor carving your drawing out of rock. Just scratch away with your pencil, making little marks until your drawing starts to look right. Remember, no one ever said it has to come out of your pencil looking perfect!

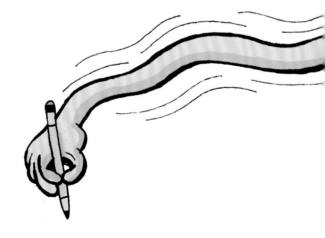

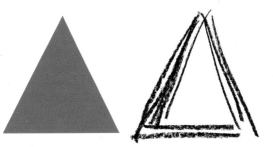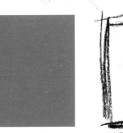

## Sketch Some Shapes

At the top of this page you can see some basic shapes. See how my sketches are loose and messy? This is how your cartoons should look at first. While sketching multiple lines, you're making tiny decisions about which line to use in the final drawing. I know this idea of sketching sounds kind of weird, but as you begin to draw more complex things, sketching will become your best friend.

What you're really doing as you lightly sketch is getting the image you have in your brain down on paper. This skill is not something we're born with. It takes practice. Remember: pencils have erasers for a reason! Don't be afraid to start out with a messy sketch. You can always clean it up later.

KEEP YOUR DRAWINGS LOOSE!!

# Heads & Bodies

When you start sketching a cartoon character, break down its body into very simple shapes. An oval for the head, and arch shape for the body, and long bendable rectangles for the arms and legs. Then, put all of these parts together to form your character's body.

# Poses

It doesn't take long to draw simple bodies in all sorts of positions. On this page, you'll see a few examples of the endless number of poses you can create with just a few simple shapes.

Stretch and bend the shapes until you get the pose you want. For balance, you should be able to draw a straight line from the cartoon character's neck, down to the supporting leg. If the neck is not aligned over the supporting foot, the character will look off balance. Draw the line as part of your initial sketch just to make sure.

BALANCE LINE

# Adding Details

After practicing some very simple-shaped bodies, add a bit of detail to them to make your characters unique. Draw them in crazy outfits. Or start with a plain round face with dots for eyes, and then add a big nose. Experiment with different styles of cartoon eyes, ears, and mouths on your drawings. The sky's the limit!

In the examples below, I started out with simple shapes and then added the details on top. In the first drawing, I wanted to end up with Santa holding a bag of toys. I had to fatten up his middle and start sketching out a beard and hat.

In the second example, I went from a generic body to a female soccer player. See how I played with the first sketch: I changed it to emphasize a thinner waist and arms, and then added some details like longer hair.

# Drawing Real Objects

See how real objects look in comparison to their cartoon counterparts? Cartoons can be much simpler and more fun to look at.

When you're drawing an object or person, it's only important to include the details most associated with that thing. You don't have to draw everything. For example, a firefighter needs a raincoat and that funny hat. That's it.

Look at some comic strips in the newspaper. Notice how artists draw complex things like computers or cars. They don't need all the details; they just need the right details to make the object recognizable.

HAT →

HOSE →

COAT →

# Cleaning Up Your Pencil Sketches

As I've mentioned before, it's important to begin drawing your cartoon very loosely so that you can work out your idea as you go.

The next step is to go over the loose sketch again with a pencil. Darken the lines that you want to keep in the final drawing and use your eraser to clean up the stray lines. This stage is called the cleaned-up or finished pencil drawing. Who knew that cleaning could be such fun?

**Rough Pencil Drawings**

**Finished Pencil Drawings**

# Inking

When you're really happy with the finished pencil drawing, it's time to redraw the cartoon in black ink. To do this, trace over the drawing in ink.

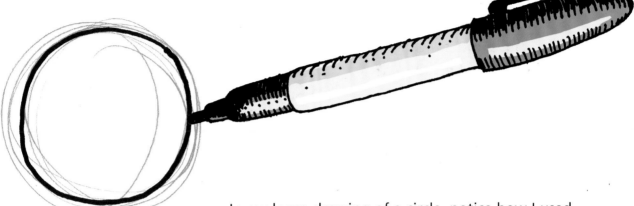

In my loose drawing of a circle, notice how I used a pen to ink over certain lines while ignoring others. During the inking stage, I made final decisions about which lines to keep and which to erase. After the ink has dried, I'll erase all of my pencil sketch lines to get a clean drawing.

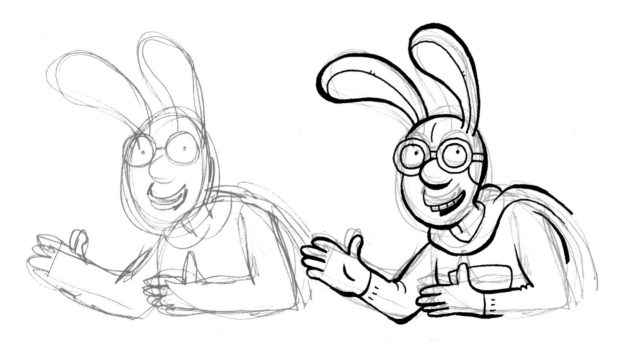

# Practice Makes Perfect!

Let's practice inking over a pencil drawing. On this page, you'll notice I've supplied some pencil drawings for you to ink. Let's pretend you did these drawings.

Using a sheet of tracing paper (don't draw in this book if it's not yours!), cover this page and trace over the drawings with your pen. The idea is not to draw over every line. Instead, only ink the best lines, the ones that look the best to you. Your finished ink drawings should have a clean, simple look to them.

If you don't have tracing paper, make a photocopy of this page. Put the copy behind a white sheet of paper. Next, hold both sheets up to a window on a sunny day. You should be able to see the pencil lines clearly through the top sheet. Now trace the ink lines onto your clean sheet.

# From Rough Sketches to Final Inks

1. Start with a very loose drawing using multiple pencil lines.

2. Darken the lines you want to be part of the finished drawing and erase the stray lines.

3. Trace the dark lines with a pen.

1.

2.

3.

# Shading and Texture

With comic strips, inking the lines is not the final step. Comic strips need shading and texture. Shading objects gives your cartoon the illusion of light and shadow. It can help show shape and volume, and it adds a good deal of interest to your drawings.

Just look around the room that you're sitting in. Everything in the room has light shining on it, casting small shadows and helping you see the shape of things. Everything has a light side and a dark side, depending on the direction of the light.

Your comic strips should have equal amounts of black and white areas in each panel. Once you figure out how much shading you like to use in your cartoons, try to stay consistent from one panel to the next with how you shade things. Shading is done with a pen in the final inking stage.

# Keep It Simple

Because cartoons are best when they're kept very simple, don't get too detailed with your shading. Use your pen to make tiny little dashes that get thicker and closer together as you get closer to the dark side of an object.

Try shading the drawings you inked on page 24. Add little shadows in the corners and fill in a few areas of black on each character. See what a difference shading makes?

It's possible to get carried away with shading, as seen in this drawing on the right. I started shading and I just couldn't stop! If you overdo your shading, a nice cartoon can quickly turn into an inky mess. Less shading is better than too much.

# Paneling

So now you know about the concepts of sketching, inking, and shading. But there's so much more to it. All comic strips are drawn inside a series of three or four squares called "panels."

I've created a design that lets me use either three or four panels per strip. Until you've written the cartoon, you're never quite sure how many panels you'll need to tell the joke or story.

I keep stacks of photocopied designs in my cartoon studio and draw my pencil roughs right on those sheets. Then I trace the finished ink drawing onto the good quality Bristol Board that I mentioned before.

On the opposite page I've provided a typical design grid for creating comic strips. With a ruler and a pencil, draw your own version of the bottom template to have as a guide when crafting your own comic strips. Using the same guide for all your comic strips will give them a more consistent, professional look.

# Paneling Guides

Lines to use as guides for lettering word balloons.

Use these notches to make a three-panel comic.

Be sure to draw your own grid at least 11 inches wide by 4 inches high. Don't forget to use a T-square.

# Chapter 3
# Getting Story Ideas

LIGHTS! CAMERA! ACTION!

Fasten your seatbelts! You're about to embark on an exciting journey. It's time to create your very own comic strip.

When you come up with characters and stories, it's as if you're a director making your own movies. You have complete control. This is my favorite thing about cartooning. There's no limit to what you can do.

Just like making a movie, creating a comic strip involves picking a cast of characters, building sets, writing dialogue, positioning your cameras, and editing scenes. You're in the director's chair from start to finish. That's what makes comic strips so much fun.

# The Story Formula

Writing comic strips is a little like writing books or movie scripts. There's a very basic formula to follow.

## CHARACTERS + SETTING = STORY

## Characters

Let your characters tell the story. Many professional cartoonists say that sometimes they just think of a situation and then let the characters react to it in their own unique ways. The writer knows exactly what that character would say in any situation.

Create a well-rounded, fully developed character with dreams, fears, and flaws. Then give that character some conflict to deal with. Your characters' reactions to conflicts will move stories along. That's what storytelling is all about.

The main character in this comic strip is a loud, headstrong young girl named Amanda DeFrancesco. She does everything big and bold, and doesn't take any guff from anyone. Create a rich, colorful personality for each of your own characters.

# Setting

Have your comic take place in an interesting location or situation. Something like a desert island, a small-town police station, or a space station on a drifting asteroid. If you decide to go with someplace less off-the-wall, such as a suburban neighborhood, be sure to invent a situation that adds an odd twist to your story. Perhaps a teenage superhero lives on the street and is trying to keep her powers and identity a secret from nosy neighbors.

Another aspect of setting is time frame. Your strip doesn't have to take place in the present. It could involve characters living in a cave thousands of years ago or robots that rule a distant planet a long time from now.

# Story

The story is the journey that your characters take. There's a beginning, middle, and end. In most books and movies, the main character has changed in some way by the end of the story after moving from start to finish.

Comic strips are a little different. The tough thing about them is that you're often creating a world that keeps going with no end in sight. Some cartoonists have drawn the same comic for 50 years—that's one long story! The world in the comic strip keeps going and going.

If comic strips don't have a big story to tell, then the characters have to do a lot of the work themselves to keep their world fresh and alive. Be sure each of your characters can help create smaller stories with the other characters in your comic.

Think about one of your favorite TV shows. If the show has a large cast of characters, sometimes the writers will pull two characters together in an episode and let them have a little story all to themselves. You should be able to do this with your cartoon characters. All together they are strong, but any two can be put together in different combinations to create fun stories.

# Let's Get Started

I promised that I would create an original comic strip as we go through this book. So here it goes!

For my strip, I'll first need to consider the things I've talked about on the previous pages: the stories, settings, time frame, and characters.

I like to start with characters. Most comics revolve around one main character who reacts to situations and becomes the center of the story.

I'll need other characters to help move the story along, too. The main character can't do it all. For your own comic strip, try to invent a cast of characters that your main character knows. The more original the central and supporting characters are, the better the strip will be—and the more fun you'll have writing jokes or telling the story.

# So What's It All About?

Okay, it's brainstorming time. This shouldn't hurt too much. So, what kind of comic strip do I feel like creating? I could place the strip in a realistic setting, like a typical suburban neighborhood. But I've been there, done that. This time I feel like doing something with more fantasy and some silly action.

Below are some ideas I've come up with. You can do this, too. On a piece of paper, list things that are interesting to you. Start with an idea for a character or with an idea for a story. It doesn't really matter which.

I try to come up with ideas that will provide a lot of story possibilities. It doesn't hurt to have a lot of options. Any of these ideas to the right could work as a comic strip as long as the characters are funny and have strong personalities.

A FUNNY COWBOY STRIP WITH A GOOFY DEPUTY FOR A MAIN CHARACTER.

A SILLY SPACE ADVENTURE WITH A DOG AS A BRAVE HERO.

A MUSCULAR SUPERHERO WITH FEAR OF HEIGHTS, CATS, AND GERMS.

A PRINCESS IN MEDIEVAL TIMES WHO WANTS TO SLAY DRAGONS.

A SARCASTIC RABBIT SHERIFF WHO KEEPS THE PEACE IN A SMALL FOREST.

A BIGFOOT WHO DECIDES TO MOVE INTO THE CITY AND GET A JOB.

I think my favorite of this bunch is the silly space adventure with a dog as the main hero. I love the idea of a guard dog in space. It's just silly and fun.

# Doodling the Dog

It's time to start drawing my space-hero dog.

When I come up with a doodle that I like, I'll study that drawing a bit and come up with a simple system for drawing that character. I like the design with the round helmet and short, stubby legs.

When you decide what kind of comic strip you want to create, just start doodling and see what comes out. Don't feel like you have to be an expert artist to design a character. A stick figure might work just fine. The sooner you decide on a drawing design, the sooner you can begin creating comics. Just keep doodling.

# A Star is Born!

I really like this design, so I'm going with it.

The combination of a cool space hero with the body of a dog is pretty ridiculous. But sometimes, when you create something very strange, it can catch people by surprise and make them laugh. In this case, I've taken two ideas—a small dog and a traditional space hero—and merged them into one hilarious character.

I'm going to call this guy "Galaxy Dog." I just like the way it sounds. In those two words I can express the silliness of the premise: a dog in space.

My drawing style is pretty simple. Most comic strips are reduced way down in size before printing. If you include a lot of details in your drawings, they can get so small that they mush together on the page. So it's a good idea to keep your characters' designs clean and simple.

# I Like Your Style

Now that I've decided on a look for my main character, how will yours look?

Every successful cartoonist has a style that makes him or her stand out from the rest of the pack. With practice, your own drawing style will develop over time. But don't worry about this too much, especially if you're not planning to publish your strip in a major newspaper.

If you're just starting out, it's okay to copy or trace other people's cartoons. That's one of the ways I learned to draw. All you have to do is keep drawing and thinking about how to make your characters' personalities appear on the page. In time, your own style will shine through. Just draw what feels natural to you and never be afraid to try new things.

To help inspire you, I've illustrated a few unique cartoon styles.

One thing to help identify your style is the height of your characters. Cartoon characters are sometimes measured in "heads." You can draw very cartoony three-head tall characters, like Galaxy Dog. You can also draw more realistic five-head tall characters. The taller the character, the more realistic his proportions will seem and the less cartoony he will be. Real people are closer to being five heads tall than they are three heads tall. Find out what you like the best and practice.

# Face Styles

Here are some samples of different styles for eyes, noses, and mouths. Just the style of mouth or nose you choose will show something about your character's personality and reflect your own, personal cartoon style. But be patient—your style will evolve over time. Before you know it, people will be able to tell a cartoon is yours.

Using a sheet of tracing paper, cover up and trace the cartoon head in the bottom corner of the page. Then practice copying the various face parts onto the blank face.

# Galaxy Dog Design 101

So, back to my Galaxy Dog character. Now that I've decided on a style and look for the character, the next thing I like to do is practice drawing him in various poses. If I'm going to be drawing a bunch of comic strips with this guy, I want him to look the same every time. Because he's a new character, it's important for me to practice drawing him. That way I'll be confident that I can draw Galaxy Dog in any situation.

I start with some basic shapes to draw my space dog. This helps me draw him the same way over and over. I've basically used a circle for a head, a small rectangle for the body, and little strips for arms and legs.

Remember loose sketching? I can relax because I know that my drawings don't have to look perfect. When I've put Galaxy Dog in the pose I want, I then begin to add the important details.

> Each of your comic-strip characters should have a slightly different shape. They shouldn't all be small and round or tall and skinny. That way, readers can easily tell your characters apart, even from far away.

1.

2.

3.

4.

# Practice, Practice, Practice

Before I start even one comic strip, I'll use up a whole stack of paper to practice drawing my main character. I'll sketch him from the front and back and from the side, standing and sitting, shooting a laser gun, maybe even floating in zero gravity.

# Supporting Characters

Can you have a comic strip with only one character? No way! You need supporting characters in any good story. So now we'll create the supporting cast for our space-hero dog. When thinking about characters for a comic strip, there are a few typical roles to consider. The first supporting roles I always think about are the sidekick, the outsider, and the antagonist.

## The Sidekick

A sidekick character gives your main character someone to talk or react to. Usually it's a best friend. If you're doing a humorous strip, make this character really nutty or weird in some way. Because my main hero is a dog, I think it would be funny to have his sidekick be a cat. Cats are usually thought of as graceful and smart, but I'm going to go in the opposite direction—I'll make my cat big and dumb. A 7-foot-tall feline with a samurai sword. Sound good? Never be afraid to try something weird with your comic strips.

NOW DIESEL — BEFORE I HIRE YOU FOR MY CREW, I HAVE TO ASK...

AS A CAT — ARE YOU GOING TO BE ABLE TO TAKE ORDERS FROM A DOG?

WHAT DOG? I THOUGHT YOU WERE A BEAVER.

# The Outsider

The outsider character in a comic strip is someone who shows up on a regular basis, but is not as close to the main character as the sidekick. The outsider usually asks a lot of questions. This character becomes very important when you try to move the story along in a strip. Because Galaxy Dog is a space story, let's make the outsider a real outsider! Let's make him a friendly alien named Joel who travels with the crew.

I came up with the name Joel because it doesn't sound like a typical alien name. The names for your characters are very important because they help set the characters apart and hopefully make them more memorable to your audience.

Joel is an advanced species and he's very civilized. He's also a bit of a weakling. He's almost the exact opposite of Diesel, the samurai cat. It's usually a good idea to make your main characters as different from each other as possible. It creates dramatic (or funny) tension and makes for better stories.

# The Antagonist

Try to think of a story that doesn't have a bad guy in it. It's hard, isn't it? Seems like bad guys, the characters you love to hate, are pretty darn important to telling a good tale.

An *antagonist* is just a fancy word for bad guy. For Galaxy Dog, the main antagonists will be mutant robots trying to take over the galaxy. With their diabolical plans, they're going to cause all sorts of trouble for Galaxy Dog and his crew. But most importantly, they'll create conflict.

Stories are all about conflict—without it, nothing exciting would happen. Conflicts can be huge events, like battles to rule the galaxy, or they can be very small problems, like someone butting in line in front of you at the grocery store. Conflict can be found anywhere, and it's essential to good writing.

# Practicing Other Characters

I did just as many practice designs for the big cat (Diesel), the alien (Joel), and the robots as I had for Galaxy Dog. When I finally settled on how they should look, I practiced drawing them in different poses.

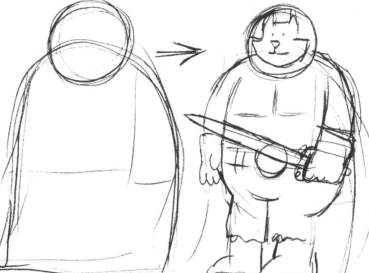

# What Makes My Characters Tick?

Do I really know my characters? To write funny stories, I have to understand my characters' personalities. Ideally, each will be quirky enough to react differently from the others to the same situation.

Think about answers to the questions on the next page for each of your characters. By doing this, you can begin to form individual personalities for your own characters. Sometimes questions like these even give you ideas for future storylines.

CUT

# Character Questions

- How would each character respond to giving a speech in front of 1,000 people?

- What does each character want most in life?

- What is each character's biggest personality flaw?

- If each of these characters had to make a choice between money and happiness, which would they choose and why?

- How would each character react to someone cutting in line in front of him?

# The Line Cutter

Let's try to answer the last personality question as an example. The characters in Galaxy Dog would all react differently to someone cutting in front of them in line. Maybe Galaxy Dog would protest and give a lengthy speech about justice and fair play. Joel wouldn't say anything to the offender, but he'd be upset and complain to his friends about it for days. Diesel would simply chop off the offender's head and go about his business.

# Story Ideas

I now know that my comic strip is going to be about this cool hero dog that defends the galaxy against mutant robots. Before I begin writing jokes, I sometimes brainstorm possible stories and situations. Below are some things I came up with. (These ideas don't have to be funny, but in this case, they should be things that could happen to a space-hero dog and his crew.)

- The mutant robots kidnap the alien, Joel.

- The crew has to reroute a meteor shower headed for a planet populated by used rocket-ship salespeople.

- The normally aggressive Diesel the Cat suddenly loses his taste for battle and becomes obnoxiously sweet.

- The crew must rid a planet of pesky (and deadly) sand beetles that accidentally infest their own ship.

- The crew must rescue a stalled imperial cruiser while a spoiled princess falls in love with Galaxy Dog (and drives him crazy).

- Joel convinces Diesel that he needs to ask Galaxy Dog for a pay raise.

- It's time for Galaxy Dog to renew his space-captain's license. He neglects to study for his test and fails.

# Asking Questions

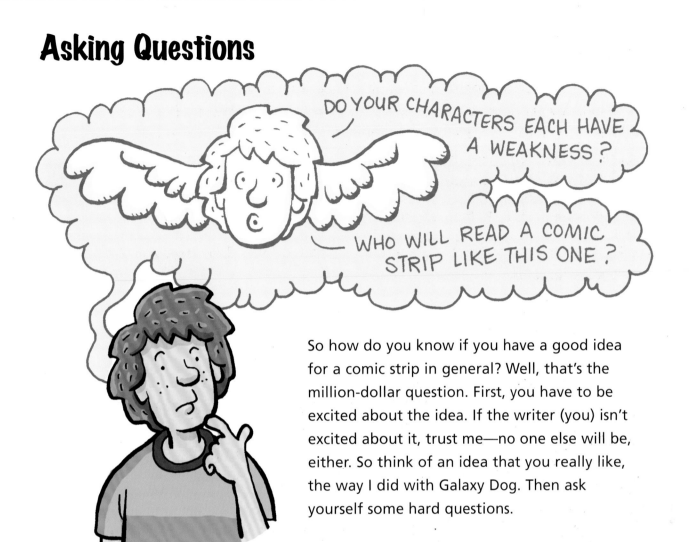

DO YOUR CHARACTERS EACH HAVE A WEAKNESS?

WHO WILL READ A COMIC STRIP LIKE THIS ONE?

So how do you know if you have a good idea for a comic strip in general? Well, that's the million-dollar question. First, you have to be excited about the idea. If the writer (you) isn't excited about it, trust me—no one else will be, either. So think of an idea that you really like, the way I did with Galaxy Dog. Then ask yourself some hard questions.

- Who would like to read a comic strip like this?

- Do all the characters have some problems? Do they have strong opinions?

- Will I be able to write stories with these characters for the next 50 years?

- Where would I like this comic strip to be published?

# Twists and Turns

Maybe you want to do a comic strip with a fairly common theme, like life at school. That's fine. Just make sure you've given your idea the odd twist it will need to stand out. Maybe your school is really a training ground for superheroes! Start with a simple idea, and then give it an imaginative spin. On this page I've listed some of the ideas I had when I was coming up with Galaxy Dog.

Evil robots who are a bunch of wimps.

a space adventure with animals

Regular Idea

My Own Twist

a cat who is a big dumb warrior.

a guard dog for the whole galaxy

# Getting Second Opinions

If you're still searching for ideas or aren't sure about the ones you already have, sometimes it helps to hear what other people think. On index cards, write your ideas for a comic strip in general or your thoughts on a storyline for an existing strip you've already created. Show your ideas to people whose opinions you trust.

Find a teacher or a family member who reads the comics every day and ask her which idea she likes. This is called "audience research." Don't worry; this isn't cheating. It's always smart to listen to people who like comics. They know what they're talking about.

It also helps to show your ideas to some friends. See which idea gets the most positive response. It might not be the one you'd have picked, but don't underestimate your friends' opinions. After all, you chose them to be your friends, so they must have something going for them!

Chances are these people might be shy about picking a favorite. They'll say, "Oh, they're all good ideas. We just think you're great, blah, blah, blah." Don't give up. Make them pick one best idea. Ask five people and see if some of them pick the same one.

What do you do if no one picks your favorite idea? Well, trust your gut and do your idea anyway. You're the boss! See? Isn't audience research fun?

# What's Everyone Else Doing?

Your next assignment is to look at the comics section in your local newspaper or on the Internet (with a parent's permission, of course). Study each strip. It always helps to know what the competition is up to. Who are the main characters in the strips you see? What is each comic about? What makes each idea different from the others? Why do you think each comic was chosen to be in the newspaper or on the website? Are there new comics featured on the page, or are they mostly older, classic comics?

Now, before we get carried away with these questions, I think it's important to say that not everyone who creates a comic strip for fun needs to worry about all this stuff. It just helps to remember the things you'll have to think about if you ever do want to be in the newspaper or online.

# Draw, Draw, Draw

Using the example of Galaxy Dog, I've shown how I approach the process of creating new characters, settings, and story ideas. Not all cartoonists work the same way as I do, but I hope you found my approach inspiring for your own cartoons.

Don't worry about how your drawings look at first. Your art will get better. If you wanted your strip to be funny, don't worry if it's not. You'll get better at that, too. The most important part of being a beginner is beginning. Just draw, draw, draw.

YOUR WORK HERE

# Chapter 4
# Writing Jokes and Stories

Okay, so you now have a great idea for a comic strip. If it's meant to be a funny strip, now's the time to start coming up with jokes and stories. No sweat! How hard could that be?

Actually...it can be pretty hard. Writing is tough work. Some days, the ideas flow like water, and you can barely write them down fast enough. But there are other times when you sit and wait for inspiration to visit you. Minutes go by, then an hour, maybe two, with nothing to show for your time.

But don't lose hope. Trust your characters and think about your story idea. The hardest part about writing is not giving up when nothing happens.

> The best way to start writing jokes for your own comic is to just start jotting down story ideas or doodling funny pictures of your characters.

FUNNY JOKE GOES HERE...

# Working For Laughs

The beauty of writing comic strips is that writers like yourself have more space to set up their jokes than they would if they were single-panel cartoonists. The punch line in a strip always comes in the last panel, and there's time to build up to it in the prior two or three panels. A story and a problem can be established before the writer moves in for the laughs.

Even more time is available for setting up jokes if a writer chooses to develop an ongoing story for his strip. Though some jokes have punch lines that are based only on character personalities and immediate situations, others also link to what's happened in the story that came before the current strip.

These two popular approaches to writing comics are called the "gag-a-day" and "story arc" techniques. Most professional cartoonists use a combination of both when they write their comics, and you can do the same if you want.

## Gag-a-Day Strips

Some comic strips are just a series of stand-alone jokes that continue day after day. Strips like these are sometimes called gag-a-day strips. Gag-a-day comic strips are meant to provide a quick laugh (a gag) but not much story. This type of writing can be more challenging because the writer must rely only on the characters instead of the stories to tell the jokes. The situations and the characters' personalities remain frozen in time, and all the jokes deal with the same kinds of subjects.

# Story Arcs

Some comic strips tell jokes based on ongoing mini-stories, like episodes on a television show. These are called story arcs. Each mini-story has a beginning and an end. Comic strips like these are almost like daytime soap operas. They can be serious or funny. The characters change and develop, and readers are pulled in to see what will happen in the next strip. Each story arc is made up of several strips that make up the full story—funny versions of these tell jokes that tie into the story being told.

# Breaking It Down

In Chapter 3, I listed a few story ideas for the Galaxy Dog strip. One of them was...

**Mutant robots kidnap the alien Joel.**

If you start with an idea like this, break the story down into a series of short events.

- THE ROBOTS NAB JOEL.
- GALAXY DOG AND DIESEL DISCOVER THAT JOEL'S MISSING.
- THEY FIND THE RANSOM NOTE.
- JOEL, TIED UP IN THE ROBOT SPACESHIP.
- GALAXY DOG AND DIESEL DECIDE HOW TO REACT.
- JOEL BEGINS TO ANNOY THE ROBOTS.

That's six day's worth of comic strips to tell the story of Joel's kidnapping. It's up to you to decide whether you want to spend a week or two months on a story. I could easily tell a bunch of jokes for each of the events listed above. Every cartoonist tells stories at his own pace.

Now let's take the first story event—the robots nab Joel. How can I make this happen in one comic strip and have it be funny at the same time?

# Brainstorming Scenarios

First, let's think about Joel's personality. He's very proper and kind of stuffy. You might say he's uptight. He's constantly cleaning the spaceship and complaining about the mess everyone's made. Plus, he's lost when it comes to using high-tech gadgets. What would be a funny way for the robots to kidnap him? I'll just try jotting down everything that comes into my head. One of these ideas might turn into a joke.

Joel goes down to planet, is ambushed

Joel mistakes the robots for vacuum cleaner

He answers the door, robots pose as salesmen.

Joel gets beamed aboard their ship.

Robot disguised as him mom

Joel gets mad and runs away.

Robots pretend they're the cleaning crew.

I like the idea that he'd mistake one of the robots for a vacuum cleaner as he's trying to tidy up the place. It fits his personality well. So now I'll try to imagine what he would say and how the action would move from one panel to the next.

# Sketching Jokes

I'll keep the kidnapping story going by sketching out jokes for the rest of the action. Here are a few of my rough sketches:

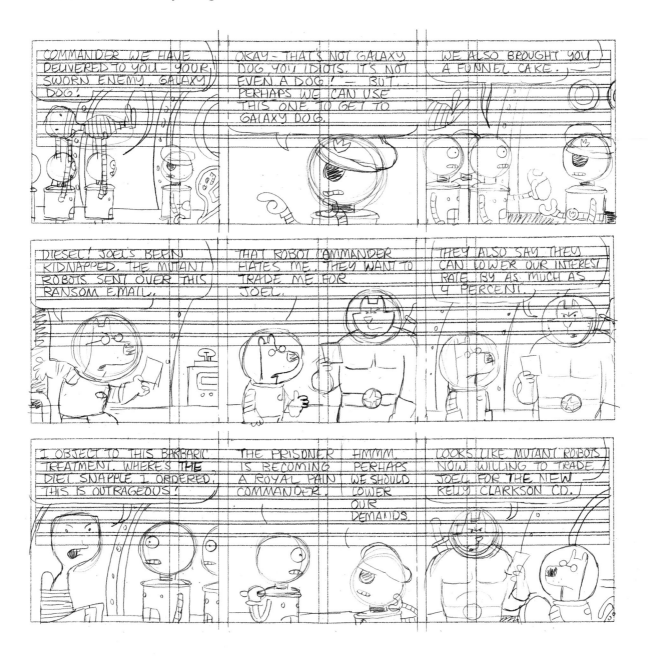

# So What IS funny?

What does it take to make people laugh? Some people are naturally funny. They have a knack of looking at the world differently than most people. Cartoonists with this gift just write and something funny appears on the page. Maybe you're lucky enough to be one of those people. Unfortunately, I'm not.

Surprise is an important tool in the cartoonist's bag of joke-writing tricks. Most people laugh at things because they didn't expect them to happen. A dog walking his owner on a leash, for example.

Another useful tool is exaggeration. Take a normal situation and get silly with it. Turn it into something that's completely ridiculous. Maybe you have a messy closet. To draw it as a comic, make it absurdly messy so that when your character opens the door, an avalanche of garbage spills out onto his head.

# Simple Steps for Making Jokes

1. Think about something funny that's happened to you or someone you know. What made it funny? Did something simple go wrong? Was anything that happened strange or surprising?

2. Now come up with an idea to start with. Like your funny memory was for you in step 1, it should start with something familiar to your audience. The simpler the better. Maybe start with a topic that revolves around the family pet, your favorite class, or the bus ride to school.

3. Now play with that idea. List everything you can think of that relates to that idea. Then come up with a list of things that are completely unrelated to it. Try combining elements of the two lists. For example, if your idea revolves around your pet dog, maybe you could write about him riding down the street on roller skates.

4. Or, exaggerate something about your idea. If something on your bus has a bad smell, make it smell so bad that the bus has to pull over so everyone can jump off it.

5. Get silly with your idea. Don't be afraid to do something surprising or ridiculous. There are no bad ideas here.

6. Take your favorite joke ideas and write them out. Start with at least four or five versions of each joke. And don't give up if it gets tough—you've come too far already!

> Remember that comic strips are meant to make people laugh, not cry. Don't use them to hurt people's feelings. Always put yourself in the place of the person reading your comic. If you feel a sting, then maybe you should go back to the drawing board.

# My Writing Routine

Most of us have to work hard at writing jokes; don't get discouraged if it's not easy for you to do. I have to be in the right frame of mind, and I can't write when my mind is occupied with something else. It's also hard for me to come up with jokes when I'm in a bad mood. The important thing to remember is to stick with it no matter how hard it gets. Don't give up!

It's also important to separate writing from drawing tasks. I may spend all day writing cartoons. The next day will be when I draw cartoons for the jokes I wrote.

When it's time to write and I'm under a deadline, I follow a pretty standard routine.

1. I think about my characters.

2. I think about something that could happen to them.

3. I list a whole bunch of weird ways to end the story.

4. I doodle a lot.

On the next page is what one of my notebook pages looks like as I'm trying to write jokes. I even keep a pad next to my bed at night in case I have a great idea in my sleep.

Captain - I've detected a meteor on a collision course with Earth.

EE Gads! ~~How long~~ How long before impact !!?

~~One~~ 343 years!

Meteors
Weather
Riots
Famine
nuke development

Hey Joel.
You too skinny.

What you eat for breakfast anyhow?

Oxygenated protein nuerons in a photon gas.

You should switch to waffles.

Gentlemen business an entr But Helping man own reward.

(blank)

and Sometimes - when I'm down on earth I steal stuff.

SOMETIMES MY SCRIBBLES ARE JOKE IDEAS, AND SOMETIMES THEY'RE JUST FUNNY LITTLE DRAWINGS TO GET MY MIND GOING.

# Roughing It Out

Now I'll draw some roughs of a few ideas. Once I have an idea that I like, I begin to rough out the comic in one of my pre-drawn grids.

Then I'll decide how many panels I'll need to create this comic strip. I'll use three.

I'll draw the dividing lines for a three-panel comic using the notches in the grid. Then I'll start penciling in the dialogue.

As you can see, I won't be winning any art contests with this drawing. It's supposed to be messy. The idea is to get the idea from my head to the paper in basic form. I can clean up the drawings later.

# Keep Your Eyes on the World

As I said at the beginning of this chapter, the most important thing about writing jokes is that you don't give up. Keep doodling, keep thinking about your characters, and watch the world around you. Every day funny things are going on. Remember to look hard and be open to ideas at any time.

1. Figure out your story.

2. Break that story down into events.

3. Exaggerate or add surprises to those events.

4. See the story through your characters' eyes—know their personalities.

Writing jokes doesn't have to be a chore. It can be an adventure. Let your imagination take off and put your characters into all sorts of crazy situations. Use ideas from the news or maybe an idea one of your friends tells you. Or take two ideas that have nothing to do with each other and put them together to form something new. Ever seen a tap-dancing elephant?

# Chapter 5
# Layout and Design

Now that we've talked about writing jokes, let's take another look at the artistic side of comics. Remember, it takes a blend of creative skills to make a great comic.

Even if you write funny jokes and create really original characters, it's usually the strip's layout and design that will catch a reader's eye on the comics page.

As I create Galaxy Dog comics, I'm making a lot of small decisions along the way. I'm deciding what style of lettering to use, how my panels will look, and from what angle to draw my characters. All of these decisions are part of layout and design.

So what makes a strong layout? In this chapter, we'll cover:

- Framing
- Camera angles
- Character placement
- Balanced shading
- Clean lettering

# Which Is Better?

Here are two examples of the same *Galaxy Dog* strip. Both comics tell the same joke. Both comics are funny (I hope). And yet, one of them looks more interesting and professional than the other. This is an example of how important layout and design can be.

A.

B.

Can you tell any difference between the two cartoons on this page? The first comic uses almost exactly the same framing in each of the three panels. This can make your comics look static and uninteresting.

The example at the bottom is the same joke, but notice the use of two medium shots on each end and a close-up of Galaxy Dog in the center. This focuses the reader's attention on the speaking character and provides some visual variety.

# What's the Time Frame?

As I've mentioned earlier, a comic strip is really a story that takes place in a little sliver of time. From the first panel to the last, the reader assumes that time is passing. What is said in the second panel happens after what is said in the first panel, and so on. It's your job to decide which images will best tell the story and how to present those images in a clear but visually interesting way.

## Passing Time

Since the time of the ancient Egyptians, artists have illustrated the passage of time by lining up a series of frames or images. Over the centuries, Western cultures

began to read the images from left to right.

Readers assume that what is shown is a story being told. Your job as cartoonist is to guide those readers step-by-step through the story in the most entertaining way. You want to hold their interest, without distracting them from the story.

From the strip above, readers aren't going to think they're seeing three Galaxy Dog clones. They know that time flows from left to right in comics. Their brains fill in the gaps between each panel and tell them that this is a picture of Galaxy Dog running toward the camera.

# Frame It

When you start sketching out the jokes you've written for your comic, pretend that you're looking through a movie camera at each frame of your comic. Design each frame to show the character that's speaking and anything else in the scene that's important to the story.

It's usually good to start with a scene that shows everything in the first frame. This sets the stage for the readers, telling them who's in the strip and identifying the setting. In movies, this is called an "establishing shot" and most directors put one in the very first shot.

The next frame usually directs the reader's eye to what is important to the story or joke. When someone is talking, you give that person a close-up. If they're holding something important, you focus on it. In the comic on this page, I had to show both Joel and Galaxy Dog to make it clear who was having the conversation.

# Far and Near

Go ahead—watch your favorite movie again. Pay attention to the opening shots. In most cases, the first thing you'll see is a faraway view shot of something like a building or a street. This is called a "wide" shot. The director is introducing you to the movie's setting. As she zooms in, you're drawn into the story, and the next thing you know, it's two hours later and the credits are rolling. Does anybody have some popcorn?

**Wide Shot**

**Close-Up**

Another shot in the director's bag of tricks is the "close-up." From that wide shot of a busy street, the camera could zero in on a small boy standing on the street looking up at the buildings. The viewer will only see this boy on the screen, perhaps just his head and shoulders. The close-up is usually a clue for the audience—somehow this boy on the street is going to be important to the story.

Many cartoonists have gone on to become movie directors because they've gotten so good at framing shots and using techniques like close-ups and wide shots. Some of the talents used to write and draw comic strips are the same as those used for movies.

# What's the Angle?

Not only can you position your imaginary camera far away from or close to your subject, but you can choose what level you want to view the scene from. By far, the most common angle used in comic strips is just from eye level, where the characters are shown straight ahead, directly even with the frame. But if you really want to mix things up, you could also move the "camera" up or down.

If you lower your camera so that you're looking up at a character, think about how big and powerful he'll look. If you raise the camera to look down, your character will appear small, maybe even helpless or afraid. Just changing the perspective of your comic-strip panel can add elements of character and emotion to the text you've written.

**Low Angle**

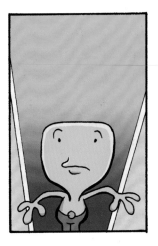

**High Angle**

And you don't always have to show your characters from the front. The camera can rotate around the scene so that you see the action from the side—or even from behind. If a character is running away from the scene, then a panel showing him disappearing into the distance from behind would be the best way to go.

**Front**                    **Back**

# Character Placement

A movie director not only has to worry about where her camera is but also where her actors stand in the scene. The same is true for comic-strip writers.

In each of the panels to the left, think about how your eyes move to the main character. I've used a little red circle to show where I want the reader to look first. What do the less important characters have in common?

A good layout not only makes a comic strip more interesting to look at, but it also determines the order in which things are read. In Western cultures, people usually read things from left to right. So, if your most important character is on the right side of each panel, the reader's eye will move across it to get to him, first taking in the scene as a whole and then focusing only on what your main character is doing or saying.

It also helps to position your less important characters lower than the main speaker in the panel. Notice how Galaxy Dog is seated next to Joel in the bottom panel on the left? Because Joel is standing, the reader automatically knows to pay more attention to him since he's speaking.

# So Many Choices...

On this page I've drawn several frame
layouts I might use in a typical Galaxy
Dog strip. By framing my characters in a
variety of camera angles and positions, I
can rearrange these panels any way I
want to tell an infinite number of jokes
or stories. Of course, for most of my
strips, I'll need to draw objects that are
important for those particular stories,
but it doesn't hurt to have a number of
layouts to start with for inspiration.

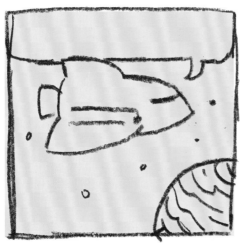

# Keep It Consistent

One thing to remember when you're changing camera angles from panel to panel or determining where to place your characters in the frame is *consistency*. Don't change things that should stay the same. For example, if a character is wearing an unusual hat in the first panel, he should still be wearing it in the second and third panels (unless there's a reason in the story for removing it) no matter what the camera angle is.

The same is true for character placement: if there's no reason for your characters to swap positions, make sure they stay where they are. Otherwise, it could be really confusing for the reader, as you can see in the strip below.

# Adding Shading to Your Design

In Chapter 2, I talked about shading a bit, but it needs to be mentioned here again because it's an important part of layout and design. Using black shaded areas in selected parts of your layout can actually guide the reader's eye from panel to panel and make the comic read more smoothly.

Shading helps show the reader what's important in the strip. It darkens the less important details of the panel and highlights the light areas occupied by central characters and objects. Because of shading, scenes can be read faster—the eye doesn't have to search the drawing to figure out what to look at.

It can also add variety to the look of the comic. Suppose each panel features two characters talking to each other. Without shading and various camera angles, the strip could look rather boring. But, if you were to show the two characters as dark shadows, or silhouettes, in the second panel, almost making it appear as if someone had turned out the lights, the contrast with the other two frames would make the strip more interesting to look at. Give it a try!

# Lettering Practice

Comic strips have always used handwritten text to show what characters are saying. Early on, it became standard practice to write dialogue in all uppercase letters. You don't have to do this—because your lettering will become part of your own style—but whichever style you choose, your text has to be easy to read.

On the opposite page, I've given you a lettering guide so you can practice adding text. Make several photocopies of this guide and practice, practice, practice! It doesn't matter what you write. Write the alphabet if you want to. The important thing is to practice making clean, legible text. Practice until your friends have no trouble reading every letter.

On page 77, I've also included examples of some common word-balloon types that you might use to show someone thinking, yelling, or even speaking from a TV broadcast. Most comic-strip readers have come to understand what these balloons mean when they see them.

At the bottom of this page, I've provided an example of lettering made with a computer. This method has become a very common way to create comic-strip text, and if you have a computer, it can save you some time and the trouble of writing everything out by hand.

# T-Squared

When drawing the boxes and lettering lines for your own comics, use a T-square to keep the lines straight and even with each other. You can get a T-square at any art supply store. You don't need a big one. A 24-inch model will do fine. Tape down your paper and use the edge of the table to line up the T-square.

For your lettering, start by drawing two horizontal lines ¼ inch apart. Then move down 1/16 inch and draw two more horizontal lines ¼ inch apart. Repeat this until you have enough lines to hold all the dialogue you want to add.

## Sound Effects

The last but not least part of comic-strip layout and design I'll mention is sound. That's right—it's time to make some noise. Sometimes you'll want to add a sound effect to your strip to make the joke funnier. Now, you won't actually be able to *hear* these sounds, but there are ways to draw them that will trick your brain into thinking you do. Below are some examples of different ways to do this.

# Chapter 6
# The Finished Comic Strip

Now that you know some drawing, writing, and design techniques for creating comic strips, it's time to put it all together. In this chapter, I'll describe my own particular way of producing a finished version of a comic strip. I'll also offer some tips and tricks I've learned during my years as a cartoonist.

Remember, you don't have to do things the way I do. All cartoonists have their own approaches. But it might be helpful for you to see the process I use to produce a finished strip. All cartoonists learn from watching others, and over the years, through trial and error, you'll develop your own methods. In the meantime, pull up a chair and look over my shoulder as I put the finishing touches on my comic strip.

# What's the Plan?

By this point I've already planned out my strip. I've decided on a story and know which characters will appear in the strip. So now it's time to make several very rough sketches of some possible layouts.

As you can see, the three versions below are exactly the same joke. I've just sketched them out as three different options. Sometimes I do this to see which one feels the best to me. After I choose the one I like, I begin drawing the first draft of the finished cartoon.

# Final Sketching

Once I begin sketching out the final cartoon, I'll use one of two methods. I'll either draw directly onto the comic panel grids that I showed you in chapter 3, or I'll begin sketching in blue pencil on good paper, and then ink the final on the same sheet.

Many cartoonists use blue pencil to sketch out the rough idea before inking in the cartoon. They use light blue pencil because it doesn't show up when the final comic is printed. Light blue is invisible to the cameras and scanners that turn the comic into a digital file.

Using blue pencil allows me to sketch and ink all on the same sheet of good quality Bristol paper. I'll still want to erase my blue lines after the ink is dry, but they won't show up as much as regular lead pencils would.

The other option is to keep all the messy sketching on cheaper stock paper. You then have to trace the sketch to create the final inked drawing on good Bristol paper. I've begun using this method more and more because I have a light box, and I find that it saves time. Either way works just fine!

# Light-Box Inking

To help me with the inking, I use a small light box that fits on a table. A light box has light bulbs inside it that shine up through a flat top made of white plastic. First, I put the paper with my first draft on the box. Then, I tape a clean sheet of high-quality Bristol Board on top of it. With the light shining through, I can see all of my messy lines on the original paper and ink the ones I like best onto the clean paper.

Because you probably don't have a light box at home, try using tracing paper or a see-through paper called vellum to do your finished ink drawings. You can get vellum or tracing paper at any art-supply store.

But, if you're serious about drawing comic strips, consider purchasing a small light box, which you can find at many art- or photography-supply stores. Prices vary depending on how nice the light box is, but you should be able to find one that is fairly inexpensive.

When I've finished tracing my strip, and I'm sure the ink is dry, I'll flip the paper over to look at my drawing in reverse on the light box. Sometimes I can catch mistakes this way that I normally wouldn't see.

CLEAN PAPER

ROUGH DRAWING

LIGHTBOX

# Brush It Up

After I do a first pass, inking the detailed areas of my drawing, I go over it again using a brush pen. I'll add thicker lines in places along my drawings' outlines.

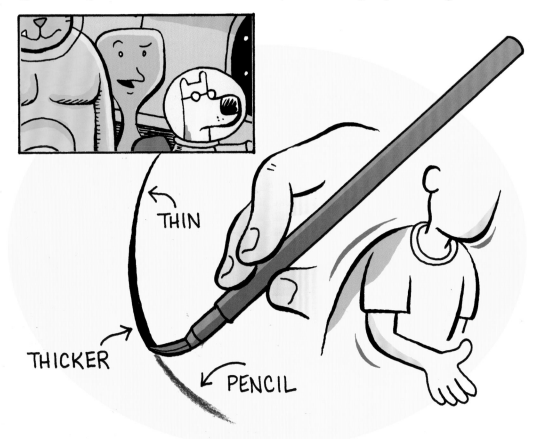

In the example on this page, I used the brush pen to make the outside lines slightly thicker around the outside curves. This takes a lot of practice, but inking your line work this way can really make a drawing pop off the page. The shapes look more round and full. I also use this technique to set the outlines apart from the interior lines. As you become a better cartoonist, study the work of the professionals and pay attention to the thick and thin lines they use to draw their cartoons. Every artist does this somewhat differently, and eventually, you'll develop your own style for inking lines.

On the next page, notice the contrast between the thick thin brushwork and the single-width lines. See how the brushwork can liven up the art? You don't even need a brush at first. Just use your pen to thicken the ink lines around corners and edges.

# Adding Black

Next, it's time to add solid black and shaded areas to your comic. See how the comic strip really jumps off the page when I add shading to it? The reader's eye will naturally go to the darkest areas, so sprinkling the comic with black shading from the first to the last frame can actually guide the reader through the strip.

For shading large areas of black, I'll sometimes use a small sable-hair paintbrush. These are available at any art store. Use a size #0, #1, or #2 for this delicate work. You don't want to slosh ink all over your comic. I gently dip the brush into a small bottle of black ink and dab it into the black areas that would be too large or tedious to fill in with a pen.

# Adding Color

If I *really* want my comic strip to get attention, I'll add some color to it.

Adding color can be a little tricky. If I'm neither using a computer nor having my comics printed in a color publication, then I have to apply color directly to the inked strip. When I do this, I always make a copy of my comic first as a precaution. By coloring on the photocopied version, the original ink drawing won't be destroyed if I should happen to mess up with the color.

I usually go all the way through the strip, applying the colors one at a time so I can make sure each is spread out in different places throughout the comic. It looks better if the reds appear evenly in each panel, and the same goes for the other colors I use. I'm going for balance. From one panel to the next, it's also important to be consistent with which color is used because comics are often repeated panels of the same scene. If a character is wearing a blue shirt in the beginning of the strip, don't change it to green by the end.

# Coloring Tools

Use colored pencils to color your work by hand, or try lightly tinted markers. If you're just attempting color for the first time, get a basic set of 24 or 48 colored pencils and a decent pencil sharpener. The average set of color markers is usually too dark for coloring comics, so pencils are the best bet. Another option is to color your work with inexpensive watercolors.

However, you should know that most artists who are starting their careers don't use color. Any photocopier can reproduce black ink lines, but color copying is expensive if your goal is to hand out a lot of copies.

# How I Color

First, I color in the larger areas, like the sky or the floor color.

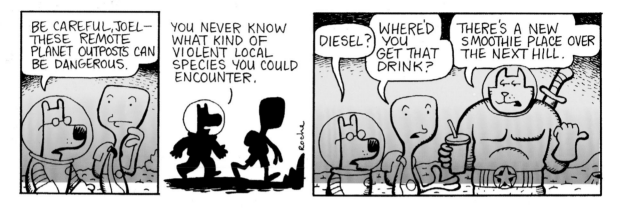

I apply the same color where it goes in each panel. Then I move on to the next color.

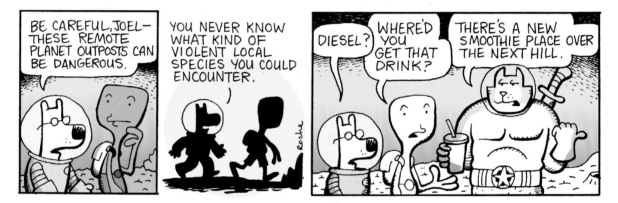

Finally, I add all the detail colors and clean up any messy coloring I've done.

# Going Digital

I have a pretty standard cartoonist's computer set-up. I use an old Macintosh computer with a scanner and a paint program. A scanner is like a photocopier for the computer. I put the cartoon face-down on the scanner. After the picture is scanned, it's stored on my computer. Then, I can use the paint program to color the comic strip.

This is really the best way to color comics because you never have to worry about messing up the original drawing. You get very pure colors, with a greater level of control over how the comic will look when it's printed. Many cartoonists not only color on a computer, they actually *draw* the comic strip on the computer. From the first rough to the finishing touches, everything is done digitally.

You might want to do your own drawings on a computer. It's all a matter of what you feel comfortable with. For me, nothing beats good old pencil and paper for the drawing part.

PEN

TABLET

SCANNER

# Coloring the Sunday Funnies

Have you ever wondered how they create the color Sunday comic strips in the newspaper? Those comics are printed on huge printing presses and sent to newspapers all over the country.

Traditionally, when a professional cartoonist is done drawing her Sunday comic, she covers the original art with tracing paper and colors in the final art on it. She then puts a little number next to each color on the tracing paper overlay. The numbers tell the printer which color to use on the final version. The numbered colors are filled in on a computer at the printer and then printed on newsprint.

These days, many cartoonists skip this process and just apply the colors themselves on their own computers. Then they send the files to the printer.

# Tell Them Who You Are!

The last little detail I add to my comic is a "byline." The byline is my signature to let people know who created the comic. Usually the byline goes in the corner of a panel somewhere. I don't want to make it too big or too small. I just neatly write my last name and today's date.

If your comic is going to be published, you'll want to substitute today's date with the date of publication.

Newspaper cartoonists put the publication dates on all their comics. Sometimes it's written very small in the corner, next to the name. By doing this, they know which comic will be running on which day of the week.

There you have it. I've just shown you how I complete a comic strip from start to finish. Now that you've seen how I do it, I hope you'll jump in and try it for yourself.

# Chapter 7
# Showing Off Your Work

So you've finished a comic strip of your very own. Now what? First, congratulate yourself. Few people actually act on the dream of creating a comic strip.

Next, don't stop there—do more! When you've created at least 12 strips, it's time to think about how you'd like to *distribute* your work. Distribute means showing your strips to a lot of people. Don't think you have to sit around and wait to be discovered by some big newspaper company looking for a cartoonist. There are many ways to get your work out there so lots of people can enjoy your creativity.

# The Comic-Strip Writers Group

Before you try to enter the publishing world, you might consider forming a writers group. This is a great way to get second opinions and advice on your work from friends and classmates who share your interest in comic strips. It's like a club. You'll meet to talk about your strips and exchange ideas about the writing and drawing process. Think of it as a test run before you hit the big time.

It's always fun to bounce ideas off people who share your interests. You might be surprised to learn that you're not the only person in your

school who likes to write comic strips. Ask your teachers or your friends if they know some fellow students who would be interested in forming a comic-strip writers group with you. Post a notice on a bulletin board and then make a list of kids who might want to join.

# Get Some Feedback

There's no one right way to run a writers group. Members could work on the same comic-strip idea or their own ideas. Either way, it's helpful to brainstorm ideas with someone else. You'll start talking about your comic strip and—before you know it—the idea is even better, all because a few people put their minds to it. Don't be afraid to seek the opinions of your fellow group mates about your comics or to give them some tips about theirs.

Be careful though. You can easily hurt someone's feelings by saying something mean about their work. Your friends are just as proud of their comics as you are of yours, so treat them the same way you'd want to be treated. Try to think of something good to say, offer some encouragement, and then mention something that might make their comics even better. Ask yourself questions while you read their comics such as:

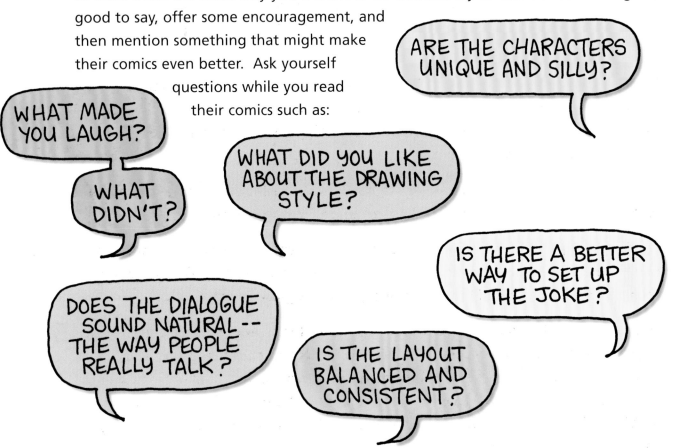

Maybe an art teacher at school will let your group meet during class time to discuss your projects. It never hurts to ask. Offer the services of your writers group to the school to do a cartoon mural or create a display in the library. It's fun to do creative projects as a team.

# Writer's Block

So, your writers group meets once a week, and for each one, you're expected to share a new comic strip with everybody. Ahhhhhhhh! The pressure!

Really, though—it's not that bad. Sure, you'll have to come up with a new idea every week, but you can do that. Imagine if you were drawing comic strips for a living. Daily newspapers expect a new strip from their cartoonists every day—even on holidays. That's 365 strips a year!

It's only natural that you'll get stuck searching for inspiration sometimes. It happens to the best of us. There are ways to get around writer's block, though.

The first thing to remember is that even though a blank page has been staring at you for the past hour, it doesn't mean that you can't cut it as a comic-strip writer. There's hope for you yet. Stand up, stretch, go get a glass of water.

Then, try to think about your comic strip from a different angle. Could you put one of your characters in a new setting, maybe someplace he hasn't been before? Remember that all stories revolve around conflict. What could happen that might cause trouble for your character in this new setting? How would he try to solve this problem? If you're having trouble coming up with a punch line, maybe try changing your setup line in the first panel.

But whatever you do, don't give up. Be patient and before you know it, a good idea will spring up out of nowhere.

# Storing Your Strips

Another great way to beat writer's block is to have a warehouse of ideas within easy reach. Try to have a special place close to where you draw that contains all of your previous comic-strip sketches and ideas. It could be a filing cabinet, a cardboard box, or whatever works best for you.

Try to keep it as organized as possible. Maybe you could sort all of your ideas by subject or characters used. The important thing is that you set up your storage system in a way that lets you find the idea you're looking for easily and quickly. You don't want to waste all of your valuable writing and drawing time digging through a pile of random papers.

Don't throw anything away. Even if you write a strip that you'll never use, file it. One day, when you're struggling for an idea, you might come across an old joke you couldn't get just right, and then, suddenly, inspiration strikes! That punch line you were searching for way back when hits you. Bye, bye, writer's block...

# Comic Strips in Newspapers

If you're ready to jump into the exciting world of publishing, where do you start? Every beginner dreams of one day getting his comic strips printed in the newspaper. But is that the best place to try first? Before you answer that, maybe it would help to know how newspapers choose the comics they run.

The comics you see in your hometown newspaper are probably appearing in more than one paper. Some are printed in hundreds of papers around the world. Each newspaper buys the comics they choose from *syndicates*. Syndicates are companies that sell feature articles, newspaper columns, photographs, and comic strips to many different newspapers at the same time. A syndicate company would try to sell your work to the newspapers. In exchange for this service, it would keep a portion of the money that the newspapers pay for your strip. These syndication companies choose only a few new comics to represent each year, so competition is extremely tough.

SYNDICATE

SYNDICATE EDITOR

NEWSPAPER EDITOR

COMICS

The list of comics most newspapers choose to publish changes very little from year to year. That makes it hard for new comic-strip writers to break into the market. It does happen occasionally, though, and those cartoonists get to earn a living doing something they truly love—drawing a daily comic strip.

# School Publications

If you're just starting out and would love to have your cartoons published, one of the best places to try is your own school publication or newsletter. Most schools have some sort of weekly or monthly newsletter. Stop by the school office and ask about contributing cartoons to the newsletter. They'll put you in touch with a teacher who can help you. Most teachers will be very open to using your cartoons as long as they aren't meant to hurt anyone's feelings.

You may even want to create a comic strip about your school. Pick topics that everyone will relate to. Maybe the school's lunches aren't very good, or maybe the mornings are crazy, with kids getting to school late. Look for subjects that you know have affected many students. Take some already silly situations and exaggerate them into crazy stories and characters.

# Local Publications

You'd be surprised at how many opportunities there are to get good cartoons published right in your own town. Think about trying church bulletins, local company newsletters, advertising flyers, restaurant menus, and free weekly newspapers. Your comics could go on one of those flyers you see posted around town on bulletin boards and telephone poles. They're a great way to let people know about community events and see your comic strip at the same time.

Consider creating a comic strip that might be perfect for a certain type of publication. Maybe your parents know someone who owns a pizza shop. You could create a comic strip about it. How about a character who is a superhero pizza chef? Get silly and let your imagination go wild. You might be able to write a comic strip that makes people want to read that publication every week. Any editor would be thrilled to add a comic that would improve readership.

# Make a Good Impression

Even though you might have just penned the greatest comic strip in the history of comic strips, it's not going to publish itself. So get out there! Let your brilliance be known. Talk to people. Tell them about yourself and ask them if they would like to look at your cartoons. When doing this in the publishing world, it's vital that you make a good impression. Here are a few tips for presenting your work:

- Do your research. Find out the name of the editor for each publication you want to approach. Call and make an appointment to show your work.

- Don't show original artwork. Instead, make clean copies so that you can leave some samples behind with each person you visit.

- Make sure your contact information (name, phone number, e-mail address) is clearly marked someplace on the cartoon so that they can contact you about doing future work.

- Show comic strips that cover subject matter specific to each publication. For church bulletins, show some strips about church parking problems or the choir. For local papers, show strips about local politics or environmental issues. It's good to keep the audience in mind at all times. Who reads the publication? What kind of comic strip would be popular with them?

- Don't be shy. Ask an adult you trust for help in contacting people. Ask them to look at your comics and give you some ideas about where to publish. Be persistent and you'll get published eventually.

# Portfolios

Presentation is everything. By this I mean that when you show people your work, you should look like a pro. If you walk into an editor's office with a comic strip scribbled on a crumpled piece of paper, it's a good bet she's not going to be very impressed.

That's why you need a nice *portfolio*. A portfolio is a portable case that contains examples of your best work. Think of it as a shop window you can carry with you wherever you go. When you want to show someone your comic strips, all you have to do is open up your portfolio and let them thumb through the pages.

As long as it's neat and clean, it doesn't matter what size your portfolio is. It could be a simple three-hole binder with plastic sleeves or a fancy leather briefcase that costs hundreds of dollars. The important thing is that your best strips are easy to see and protected from fingerprints and dirt. You might also stash copies of your work in a folder or pocket within your portfolio so samples can be left with people who are interested in what you do.

MY COMIC BY me 555-1234

# Websites for Comic Strips

There are hundreds of places on the Internet that post cartoons and comic strips. After you get permission to surf the Web, use search engines to find websites that post "kids cartoons" or "kids comic strips." Look for websites that accept comics sent in from kids. Some of these even have sections that allow users to create *blogs* to go with their comic strips. A blog is short for an Internet log, and it's basically an online journal that you can write in and update as often as you like. Some sites let you create your own page, posting comics and your blog in the same place. This is the online equivalent of self-publishing.

If there is a website that covers a subject that interests you, you can send an e-mail to the webmaster, or person who created the site, and offer to do a regular cartoon for it.

Maybe your soccer team has a website. You could do a comic strip about your team. If you're really into trading-card games, perhaps a website is out there that would love to feature a funny strip. Just think about a subject that interests you and create a comic strip about it.

## Attention Parents!

Be sure to monitor the websites your children visit. Some cartoon websites can contain comic strips that are inappropriate for minors. Look for art sites that encourage kids to send material. Check the material that has been submitted to it, as well as the tone of the website, to make sure the content is appropriate for your child.

# Publishing on the Web

In order to post your comics online, you'll have to convert your artwork into digital files that can be sent through e-mail. This is done with a computer scanner. A scanner is like a copy machine, but instead of a paper copy, it creates a digital file on a computer. If you don't have a computer with a scanner at home, ask a teacher if you can use one at school. Get help using the software for scanning images. Once you've made a digital picture of your comic strip, it's easy to send the digital file to a website for posting.

Publishing your comic strips on the Internet is becoming more common. However, don't expect to make a lot of money doing it. Though it's easy to reach a large number of readers by using the Internet, most of the content provided is now free. Only a tiny percentage of the public is willing to pay money for online comics.

# Contests

Some art contests accept comic-strip entries. You could get some attention for your comic and maybe even win a prize! The art teacher at your school might have some information about contests in your area. Check your local newspaper or take a look at the bulletin boards in local art schools for art contest announcements.

With the help of your art teacher, you could organize your very own cartoon contest. Pick a topic that everyone knows about. It could be a news item or something fun like coming up with the best superhero design. Create flyers and put them around your school. Ask for submissions and give a deadline for turning in artwork. Ask a few teachers to judge the contest and to help you come up with some fun prizes. Contests can draw a lot of attention to your comics, and they can be a lot of fun, too.

Someone at your local newspaper may also know about some contests for young cartoonists. Call and ask to speak to an editor in the "features" department. These are usually the folks that deal with the daily cartoons, and sometimes they'll know about a national contest one of the big cartoon syndicates is offering. If you find contests like these, enter all of them. It's good experience.

# Or...Just Do It Yourself!

The great thing about being a beginning cartoonist is self-publishing. The easiest way to self-publish is to go to your local copy shop and start running off copies of your comics.

First, use the photocopier to shrink your comics down to a size that will let you fit three on an 8½ x 11-inch page. Cut and paste them onto the paper and make 20 sets of the 12 comics you did. Hand them out to friends, teachers, Mom, Dad, and even crazy Uncle Larry. Let everyone see how brilliant and funny you are. You might even want to attach a short, one-page description of your comic-strip idea, which includes a few sentences describing each main character.

# Other Self-Publishing Ideas

There are so many ways to publish funny comic strips, it's impossible to cover them all in one book, let alone in one chapter!

The ideas that follow are not only great ways to get your ideas out there, but they can make great gifts for friends and family, too.

## Comic Strip Books

Create entire books of your comic strips. This way you can show more story than if you were to publish your comics one at a time.

Using sheets of 8½ x 11-inch paper, shrink your comics on a photocopier so that they fit three to a page. Then, paste the small strips onto your paper on the front and back. Number your pages. If your comic strips tell ongoing mini-stories, make sure that you paste them in order on your pages.

Don't forget to create a full-color cover for your comic book. You could use two sheets of construction paper that are slightly larger than the inside pages. Once you've decorated the cover with characters from your strip, staple the binding together or punch holes along the left edge and tie the pages together with yarn or string. Or get even fancier: an office-supply store can help you assemble your book, too.

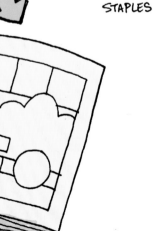

STAPLES

COVER

# Greeting Cards

Greeting cards are a great way to showcase your comics. Think about it: how long do holiday or birthday cards sit on your parents' shelf? A few days? A week? A month? Long enough for visitors to notice and say, "Wow, what amazing talent!"

Copy a strip or two onto heavy paper and fold it in half so it opens up like a greeting card. Decorate cards with a holiday/birthday version of one of your comic strips. Hand-color your cards using colored pencils. Find envelopes and send the cards out to family and friends.

# T-Shirts, Calendars, Etc.

You don't need to wait for someone else to promote your work. Do it yourself. Create a monthly newsletter for family and friends. Include not only news and feature articles you and others have written, but also have a whole page devoted to nothing but comic strips.

With a simple publishing program on your computer, you can create calendars that will hang on some lucky person's wall all year. That's a month of display time for each comic you include.

If you have digital files of your comic strips, create coffee mugs, calendars, T-shirts, and all sorts of gift items by using Internet sites that charge money for printing small numbers of items with the artwork that you provide. One website like this is www.cafepress.com.

A publishing program can also help you make T-shirts—or as I call them: walking comic-strip billboards. Buy some transfer paper for your printer, print your comic on it (don't forget to flip the image first), and then get an adult to help you iron the image onto a plain T-shirt.

Have fun and get your comics out there for people to see!

# How to Improve

Nobody's perfect. I've been in the comic-strip business for a long time, but I'm still finding ways to improve. You should, too.

Always keep an eye on what other artists are doing: read the daily and Sunday comics, visit popular (and parent-approved) comic-strip websites, buy book collections of your favorite strips, and study the competition wherever you see it—even in the greeting-card section of the grocery store.

Take art classes during or after school (your art teacher should be able to help you find good ones).

Ask for advice from experts. There are many other cartoonists out there like me who are more than happy to offer tips and tricks of the trade. Seek them out. Pick their brains. Learn from them.

Publish, publish, publish. Your work doesn't have to appear in a national newspaper. In fact, most famous cartoonists got their starts in local publications. Try presenting your strips in a variety of forms, whether it's in a church bulletin or on a birthday card. Remember, the more eyes that see your work, the better your chances are of making the big time.

Most importantly, DON'T be afraid of rejection. Take it as a challenge to do better work. There are a lot of comic-strip artists out there making a living doing what they love, and if you keep at it, one day you'll be doing the same.

# Final Thoughts

In this book, I've tried to cover all the bases for creating your own comic strips. One of the reasons I love the art of comic strips so much is that it provides more challenges than a single person could ever master in a lifetime.

I hope you've enjoyed this journey as much as I did. My goal was to make it easier for you to get started. Follow the simple steps in this book and work toward becoming a professional cartoonist. Or, just create comics for fun! Follow your own path and don't give up. All you need is the desire and the drive (together with the small jumpstart I hope this book provides), and you're on your way. So, from Galaxy Dog, Diesel, Joel, and me, goodbye and happy cartooning!

# Appendix: Interview with a Comic-Strip Editor

For the inside scoop on how comics get chosen for local newspapers, I sat down to chat with *Atlanta Journal Constitution* editor Frank Rizzo.

**What do you look for when you're hunting for new comics?**

Is it different from other strips? Is it well-drawn? Does it make readers laugh? Does the strip target a different group of readers than most other strips?

I see a lot of comics that are pretty much like established comics; the characters and situations are different, but the humor is much the same. I don't want to pick comics that are just like the ones we already have; I want different ones.

I don't pick comics for the newspaper just because I like them. We run several comics that I don't particularly care for, but I know that there are many readers who do like them. My job is to make sure the newspaper runs a variety of comic strips so that every reader will find at least a few to like. And that's not easy!

**Where do you get the comic strips that you buy?**

Newspapers buy their comics from features syndicates. These are companies that offer a variety of material to newspapers, from columnists and cartoons to crossword puzzles and horoscopes. By selling a cartoonist's work to many newspapers for a small amount, a syndicate makes it possible for each paper to afford a range of comics—and by maximizing sales, a cartoonist can earn a living wage.

A syndicate will help a cartoonist develop her strip, edit it, sell it to newspapers, and make sure it's sent out on schedule.

**Do you have any advice for someone creating his very first comic strip?**

Don't start drawing a comic because you want to become a rich and famous cartoonist. That almost never happens!

Create a comic because you love to draw and it's fun to share your work with readers. You'll never be disappointed! (And if your comic is enjoyed by many other readers, success will find you.)

# Acknowledgments

I'd like to acknowledge the hard work of Wolf Hoelscher, Joe Rhatigan, Robin Gregory, and Celia Naranjo at Lark Books. Together we all battled through crazy deadlines, writer's block, and many rewrites. A great big thanks to my wife, Elizabeth, and my two very understanding boys. They spent months having to tip toe past my studio while I was writing this book.

I dedicate this book to the person who gave me my name, my dad, Arthur F. Roche Jr. He introduced me to the first real cartoonist I ever met. Then he made me believe that one day I could be one, too.

# Recommended Reading

Because it's a subject so rich in history and influences, there are many other books that you should read to gain a broader view of the art form. I've listed a few of the books that have influenced me over the years.

*The Best of Hi and Lois*, by Mort Walker, Dik Browne, and Brian Walker (iUniverse, 2005).

*The Comics: An Illustrated History of Comic Strip Art*, by Jerry Robinson (Dark Horse, 2006).

*The Comics Before 1945*, by Brian Walker (HNA Books, 2004).

*The Essential Calvin and Hobbes: A Calvin and Hobbes Treasury*, by Bill Watterson (Andrews and McMeel, 1988).

*Peanuts Treasury*, by Charles Schulz (Barnes & Noble Books, 2000).

# Metrics

Need to convert inches to centimeters? It's simple: just multiply by 2.5.

# Index